Gut vs. Grind

Master Your Decision-Making Systems

Freudian Trips

Copyright Page

Disclaimer

The views and opinions expressed in this book are those of the author(s) and do not necessarily reflect the official policy or position of any other agency, organization, employer, or company. The contents of this book are for informational and educational purposes only and are not intended to serve as professional advice, diagnosis, or treatment.

The information provided in this book is believed to be accurate and reliable as of the date of publication. However, it may include some errors or inaccuracies, and no warranty or guarantee is provided regarding the accuracy, timeliness, or applicability of the content.

Readers are encouraged to consult with professional philosophers, educators, or other qualified professionals where appropriate for personalized advice. The author(s) and publisher shall not be liable for any loss, damage, or harm caused or alleged to be caused, directly or indirectly, by the information or ideas contained, suggested, or referenced in this book.

By reading this book, the reader acknowledges and agrees that they are solely responsible for how they interpret and apply the information contained herein.

This book may also include references to other works, studies, and sources. These references are provided for further reading and exploration and do not imply endorsement or validation of the specific theories, viewpoints, or interpretations presented in those works.

Introduction: The Tug-of-War in Your Head

Heart vs. Head

Have you ever bought something on a whim, only to regret it a few hours later? Or maybe you fell head-over-heels for someone, even though your friends warned you they were trouble? How about those moments struggling between eating that extra slice of cake and sticking to your diet? These are all classic signs that you're caught in the never-ending battle between heart and head.

See, we humans like to think of ourselves as logical creatures. We make lists, weigh pros and cons...we plan. But often, just when we think we have it all figured out, a powerful feeling swoops in and throws a wrench in our carefully crafted plans. It turns out we don't have one brain – we have two!

Your Two-Speed Brain

Scientists and philosophers have been fascinated by this idea for centuries. How can we be so rational yet so impulsive at times? Modern psychology has given us a fascinating answer: the Dual Process Theory. In a nutshell, it means you have two thinking systems constantly operating inside your head:

- **System 1: The Speedy One** This is your fast, automatic, go-with-your-gut brain. It relies on instinct, experience, and emotion. It makes snap judgments and helps you react quickly to the world.
- **System 2: The Thoughtful One** This is your slow, logical, and deliberate brain. It's the voice that reasons things out, plans for the future, and tries to keep your impulses in check.

A Brief History of the Mind's Tug-of-War

People haven't always thought of the brain this way. Early philosophers saw pure reason as the pinnacle of being human. Emotions were seen as messy and disruptive! But as scientists began to study how we *really* think and make decisions, it became clear that things are way more complicated.

Modern psychology picked up this thread. Researchers like Daniel Kahneman (author of the famous book "Thinking, Fast and Slow") revealed just how much of our mental lives happen without our conscious awareness. This idea of two thinking systems gives us a way to understand why we sometimes feel so conflicted!

Up Next

Now that you know the basics, it's time for the fun part. Over the next few chapters, we'll take a deep dive into each of these systems. We'll look at how they help us (and sometimes get us into trouble). Most importantly, you'll learn some tools to help these two sides of your brain work together to make your life smoother and your decisions a lot wiser!

Chapter 1: Your Brain on Autopilot

Think of your System 1 brain like the autopilot feature on a plane. With autopilot on, the plane can fly pretty much by itself, reacting to weather patterns, making adjustments, all without the pilot constantly tweaking the controls. Your System 1 brain works a lot like that, running the show most of the time without you consciously having to think much about it.

What System 1 Does Best

Here's where this fast, autopilot brain really shines:

- **Everyday Habits:** Think about brushing your teeth or driving your usual route home. System 1 has learned these so well they feel almost automatic.
- **Reading Emotions:** That flash of understanding when you see a friend's frown, even before they say anything? That's your System 1 picking up on their emotional state instantly.

- **Quick Reactions:** See something hurtling towards you? Your dodging out of the way is pure System 1, saving you before you even process what's happened.

Survival of the Fastest

System 1's superpower is speed. Back when our ancestors roamed the savannahs, it wasn't about crafting five-year plans, it was about dodging hungry predators and spotting edible berries *fast*. Those with quick-thinking System 1 brains were more likely to survive and pass on their genes (that's you!).

Gut Feelings: Should You Trust Them?

This is where things get interesting. System 1 intuition, or those gut feelings, can be incredibly helpful...and sometimes totally misleading.

- **Good Gut:** You meet someone for the first time and they seem... *off*. You don't know why, but you get a bad vibe. System 1 excels at picking up on subtle cues others might miss.
- **Bad Gut:** The dessert table looks incredible, and that inner voice says, "Eat it ALL!" That voice is often driven by cravings and short-term pleasure, not what's best for you long-term.

Understanding Your Autopilot

The key thing about System 1 isn't whether it's good or bad, but understanding how it works. Sometimes your intuition is dead-on, other times your instincts lead you astray. Noticing the patterns of when your gut is a helpful guide versus a hungry troublemaker is powerful knowledge.

Up Next...

Your fast-acting System 1 keeps life humming smoothly most of the time. But, there are those big decisions and complex problems where you need some slower, more careful thinking. That's where your System 2 brain comes in – and we'll meet that thoughtful character in the next chapter!

Chapter 2: When Slow and Steady Wins the Race

Remember that feeling of straining over a tough math problem in school, brow furrowed, that 'aha!' moment finally clicking? That's your System 2 brain in action. Unlike your speedy, automatic System 1, this brain mode is all about focus, logic, and carefully considering the facts at hand.

System 2: Your Mental Muscle

Think of System 2 as the weightlifter compared to System 1's sprinter. Here's what it's good at:

- **The Long Game:** Planning a big trip, saving for a house, learning a new language...none of these happen overnight. System 2 lets you set goals and devise step-by-step plans to reach them.
- **Wrestling with Choices:** Should you take that new job offer? System 2 helps you weigh the pros and cons, analyze facts, and make well-reasoned decisions.

- **Taming the Beast:** Remember those tempting desserts System 1 wanted to devour? System 2 is the voice reminding you of your health goals and helping you exercise willpower.

Why Deliberation is Awesome

System 2 is what has made humans so incredibly adaptable. It's what allows us to build skyscrapers, cure diseases, and create amazing art. When faced with new challenges, it's your rational, problem-solving mind that steps up to the plate.

When Your Brain Gets Tired

The downside of System 2 is that it takes serious mental energy. Have you ever felt mentally wiped out after a long day of intense studying or decision-making? That's your System 2 getting worn down. This is where those thinking pitfalls come in:

- **The Shortcut Trap:** Our brains are built to conserve energy. Sometimes, System 2 gets lazy and looks for shortcuts. Instead of careful analysis, we start relying on stereotypes or assumptions that can lead to bad decisions.
- **Information Overload:** In a world with endless news and opinions, System 2 can get overwhelmed. Too much data can paralyze us, making it harder to focus on what really matters.

Training Your Thinking Muscle

The good news is, like any muscle, System 2 can be strengthened! Here's how:

- **Embrace the Challenge:** Tackle puzzles, learn new skills... things that force your brain to slow down and work hard.
- **Question Everything:** Don't just accept information at face value, especially if it plays into your emotions. Practice critical thinking!
- **Mindful Breaks:** Just like athletes need rest, System 2 needs a break occasionally. Meditating or walking in nature helps reset your mental energy.

Up Next

Systems 1 and 2 are both super valuable, but the real magic happens when they work together. Sometimes, that involves a little friendly wrestling! We'll dive into the tug-of-war between your intuitive and analytical minds in the next chapter.

Chapter 3: Caught in the Crossfire

Imagine your brain is a bit like a parent-child duo. System 1 is the impulsive child, always wanting what it wants *right now*. System 2 is the more patient, reasonable parent, trying to steer things in the right direction. Most of the time, they coexist okay...but sometimes, the fireworks start!

Classic Clashes

Here are some everyday battlegrounds where your two brains often duke it out:

- **The Battle of the Snooze Button:** The alarm blares. System 1 whines, "More sleep!" while System 2 groans, knowing you'll feel terrible if you're late.
- **Impulse Buys:** You see those shiny new shoes, and System 1 says, "MUST HAVE!" System 2 faintly whispers about budgets, but often gets drowned out.
- **Social Drama:** A friend says something hurtful. System 1 wants to lash out in anger, while System 2 tries to urge a calmer response, but that takes time.

When Emotions Take the Wheel

Things get really messy when strong emotions are involved. Imagine your emotions like a sudden storm. System 2, your rational pilot, gets blown off course as System 1 instincts take over. This is that "seeing red" feeling when it's almost impossible to think straight:

- **Road Rage:** Someone cuts you off in traffic, and blind anger makes you do something reckless.
- **Love at First Sight:** You meet someone, and all logic goes out the window. System 1 is swept away with infatuation, ignoring any potential warning signs.

Do You *Really* Choose Your Thoughts?

This tug-of-war leads to a big question: are we really in charge of our minds? If lightning-fast System 1 is constantly reacting and sending impulses, how much conscious control do we actually have?

Philosophers and scientists have debated this for ages. Some believe our choices are an illusion, the result of fast brain processes we don't fully understand. Others argue that System 2, though slow, is where true willpower and self-determination lie.

The Take-Away

There's no easy answer about free will. But recognizing this internal push-and-pull is a huge step. Instead of feeling like a victim of your own brain's whims, you can start to become an observer:

- **Notice the Triggers:** What situations usually lead to System 1 taking over? Stress, hunger, certain people?
- **Question Those Impulses:** When you feel that strong urge, ask yourself, "Is this really what I want, or is this my brain on autopilot?"

Next Up...

There's no winning this brain battle by trying to get rid of one side or the other. Real power comes from getting Systems 1 and 2 to work as a team. We'll look at how to do that in the next chapter!

Chapter 4: Become Your Brain's Coach

Think of your two thinking systems as star athletes on a team. System 1 is the speedy, flashy one with raw talent. System 2 is the powerhouse with strategy and determination. A good coach doesn't get rid of either player; they train them both to harness their strengths and work together to win!

Training Your Inner Sherlock Holmes

Your gut feelings (System 1) can be valuable, but also unreliable. Here's how to know when to trust them:

- **Know Your Turf:** Intuition is often more accurate in areas where you have experience. That uneasy feeling about a new acquaintance might be off, but that same feeling about an investment you understand well deserves attention.
- **Beware of Bias:** System 1 often falls for stereotypes and past negative experiences. Notice if a 'gut feeling' seems more rooted in fear or prejudice than genuine insight.

- **The Body Test:** Intuition sometimes shows up as a physical feeling. A good hunch might feel like a warm 'yes', while a wrong path might give you butterflies or a tight chest.

Sharpen Your Critical Thinking Sword

To make the most of your rational System 2, try these mind-strengthening workouts:

- **The 5 Whys:** Like an annoying kid, keep asking "why?" to get to the root of a problem. "I'm feeling stressed" ...Why? "Too much work"... Why? (keep going!)
- **Play Devil's Advocate:** Force yourself to argue the opposite of what you believe. This busts thought bubbles and helps spot flaws in your own reasoning.
- **Embrace Being Wrong:** Nobody likes it, but mistakes are the best teachers. Instead of getting defensive, analyze *why* you thought something was true, and how to find better info next time.

The Power of Doing Nothing (for a Moment)

The biggest weapon against System 1's impulsiveness is surprisingly simple: Pause.

- **Mini-Meditations:** Even 5 minutes of focusing on your breath calms the emotional storm and allows System 2 to kick in. Plenty of apps can guide you if you're new to this.
- **The 10-Second Rule:** Before reacting to anything, literally count to 10. It seems silly, but it can work wonders in letting your wiser self take the lead.

- **Walk it Out:** Physical movement shifts your mental
  state. If you're stuck on a decision, a walk around the
  block can bring surprising clarity.

The Takeaway

This brain training is a lifelong process, not an overnight fix.
Some days, System 1 will run wild. That's okay! The more you
practice noticing and understanding how your mind works, the
less it will control you, and the more control you'll gain.

Up Next...

Now that you've got some tools to work with, let's put them
into practice! In the next chapter, we'll look at how to use both
your intuition and logic to tackle real-life problems, from
relationships to finances, and everything in between.

Chapter 5: Your Thinking Systems in Action

Okay, enough theory! It's time to see how this mind stuff helps you with actual problems we all face:

Relationships: Heart & Head in Harmony

- **Emotional Decoding:** System 1 picks up on subtle cues: a partner's distant tone, a friend's forced smile. Don't ignore these, but use System 2 to ask, "Am I reading this right? Or is my past/stress talking?"
- **Conflict with Compassion:** Anger wants to lash out, but System 2 reminds you of your long-term goal (a harmonious bond). Take a time-out if needed, then come back to discuss calmly.
- **Spotting Red Flags:** Intuition about a new person can be lifesavers. But don't let System 1's fears sabotage good things – analyze those gut feelings rationally before jumping to conclusions.

Money Matters: Outsmart Your Impulses

- **Budget Battles:** System 1 craves instant fun (shopping spree!), System 2 sees the long game. Write out your big financial goals to keep that future vision strong when temptation strikes.
- **Don't Be Fooled:** Sales tactics prey on System 1's "must-have-now" mentality. The 24-hour rule (waiting a day before big purchases) lets System 2 catch up and ask, "Do I really need this?"
- **Investing Intelligently:** The hype around the hot new stock is tempting, but System 2 does the research and focuses on slow, steady growth.

Health: Kicking Bad Habits, Building Good Ones

- **Willpower Workout:** Resisting that extra slice of cake is a System 2 flex! Breaking big goals into tiny steps ("Just walk for 10 minutes") tricks your brain into getting started.
- **Habit Hacking:** System 1 thrives on routine. Make healthy choices easy (prepped snacks on hand) and temptations harder to reach (junk food out of sight).
- **Self-Compassion, Not Self-Sabotage:** Messing up happens. Instead of System 1 berating you, let System 2 analyze *why* you fell off track and how to prevent it next time.

Workplace Wisdom

- **Don't React, Respond:** That annoying email from a coworker? Pause before firing back. System 2 helps you craft a strategic response that doesn't escalate the situation.

- **The Team Builder:** A good leader taps into both System 1's intuition about people's strengths and System 2's analysis of data and strategy.
- **Decision Time:** For big calls, gather info, analyze, but also let it simmer. Sometimes your subconscious System 1 processes things even when you're not actively thinking.

Remember: It's a Journey

No one has their thinking systems perfectly balanced all the time. Some days it takes all your willpower to resist that donut, others you nail a tough financial choice with ease. The important thing is awareness. The more you notice which mental mode is dominating, the better equipped you are to make the choices that truly serve you!

Conclusion: The Thinking Team of the Future

Throughout this journey, we've uncovered the secret world of your two-speed brain. It might seem messy and confusing at times, but there's a beautiful power in this internal dance of intuition and analysis. The key isn't trying to force one system to always rule, but creating a partnership.

Embracing the Whole Team

Imagine your mind like a top sports team. You wouldn't just want slow, strategic players, nor would you want only impulsive speedsters. You need both, each playing to their strengths at the right times for the win. That win, in this case, is a life filled with smarter decisions, better relationships, and achieving the goals that truly matter to you.

Mistakes are Mentors

We all have those moments where System 1 led us astray – the impulse buy, the harsh words we regret. We also have those times where overthinking paralyzed us or stopped us from taking a good, calculated risk. Don't beat yourself up! Mistakes offer some of the most powerful lessons. Analyzing *why* you decided the way you did illuminates your unique mental habits. This self-awareness is your secret weapon for making better and better calls in the future.

The Mind of Tomorrow

It's a crazy exciting time to be thinking about thinking! Neuroscience is constantly uncovering new secrets about how our brains work. Artificial intelligence is showing us a different kind of decision-making altogether. These fields may hold the key to enhancing our own mental abilities:

- **The Brain Whisperer:** Imagine a future where technology could give you real-time feedback on when System 1 is hijacking your better judgment or when System 2 is stuck in a loop.
- **AI Assistants:** AI is already outsmarting us in certain tasks. Could collaboration with super-smart AI give us access to a kind of expanded System 2, processing information and spotting patterns the human mind alone cannot?

The Takeaway

Whether the future brings mind-reading gadgets or not, the most amazing thinking tool is the one you already have. By understanding how your two thinking systems operate, the more you become the master of your own mind. The future of smarter, wiser decisions starts with you, right here, right now.

Invitation to Explore

This book has been a starting point, but the exploration of your mind is endless! If any of the topics sparked your curiosity, here are some ways to keep learning:

- **Books on Behavioral Economics:** Dive into the fascinating ways our brains often make predictably irrational choices when it comes to money (a great example is *Thinking, Fast and Slow* by Daniel Kahneman).
- **Meditation & Mindfulness:** There's growing scientific support for how these practices enhance self-awareness and mental control.
- **Philosophy of Mind:** If the free will question intrigues you, delve into the works of great thinkers debating this for centuries!

The journey to understanding your own mind is one of the most rewarding you'll ever take. Wishing you all the best on your adventures in thinking!

About Freudian Trips

Welcome to Freudian Trips, your dedicated platform for diving deep into the world of psychology. We are more than just a YouTube channel or a book publisher. We are a beacon of enlightenment, making complex psychological concepts accessible and engaging for all.

Our YouTube channel is a rich repository of psychology made simple. We take the profound and often complex ideas from the world of psychology and break them down into digestible, easy-to-understand content. From the foundational theories of Freud to the cognitive insights of Piaget, we cover a broad spectrum of psychological schools and thoughts, making psychology accessible to everyone, regardless of their background or prior knowledge.

As a book publisher, we take the same approach, transforming intricate psychological theories into comprehensible narratives. Our books are not just collections of words, but vessels of wisdom that make psychology approachable and relatable. We believe that psychology should not be confined to academic circles, but should be available to all who seek to understand the human mind and behavior.

At Freudian Trips, we believe in the power of curiosity and the pursuit of knowledge. We are here to stoke the fires of your curiosity, to guide you on your intellectual journey, and to help you navigate the fascinating world of psychology.

If you are someone who is not afraid to question, to explore, and to learn, then you are in the right place. Join us on this journey of exploration, as we make psychology easy to understand, one concept at a time.

Be sure to visit our Youtube channel at:
www.freudiantrips.com/youtube

You can also visit us on the web at www.freudiantrips.com

Welcome to The Freudian Trip community. Stay curious. Stay enlightened.

www.ingramcontent.com/pod-product-compliance
Lightning Source LLC
Chambersburg PA
CBHW072346270726
48659CB00023B/2417